For you,

who will never

be further away

than my heartbeat.

You know who you are.

Forever

Flavia and Lisa Weedn

Illustrated by Flavia Weedn

Cedco Publishing Company · San Rafael, California

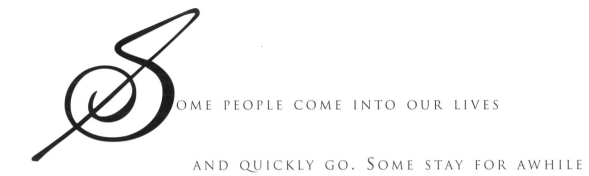

Some people come into our lives

and quickly go. Some stay for awhile

and embrace our silent dreams.

E HEAR THE MUSIC THEY HEAR

AND UNDERSTAND

THE ETERNAL RISING

OF ITS POETRY.

THEY HELP US BECOME AWARE

OF THE DELICATE WINDS OF HOPE,

AND WE DISCOVER THAT WITHIN EVERY HUMAN SPIRIT

THERE ARE WINGS YEARNING TO FLY.

Because we have been touched

by the strength and beauty

of another soul,

we own new-found courage.

THEY HELP OUR HEARTS TO SEE THAT

THE ONLY STAIRWAY TO THE STARS IS WOVEN WITH DREAMS,

AND WE FIND OURSELVES UNAFRAID TO REACH HIGH.

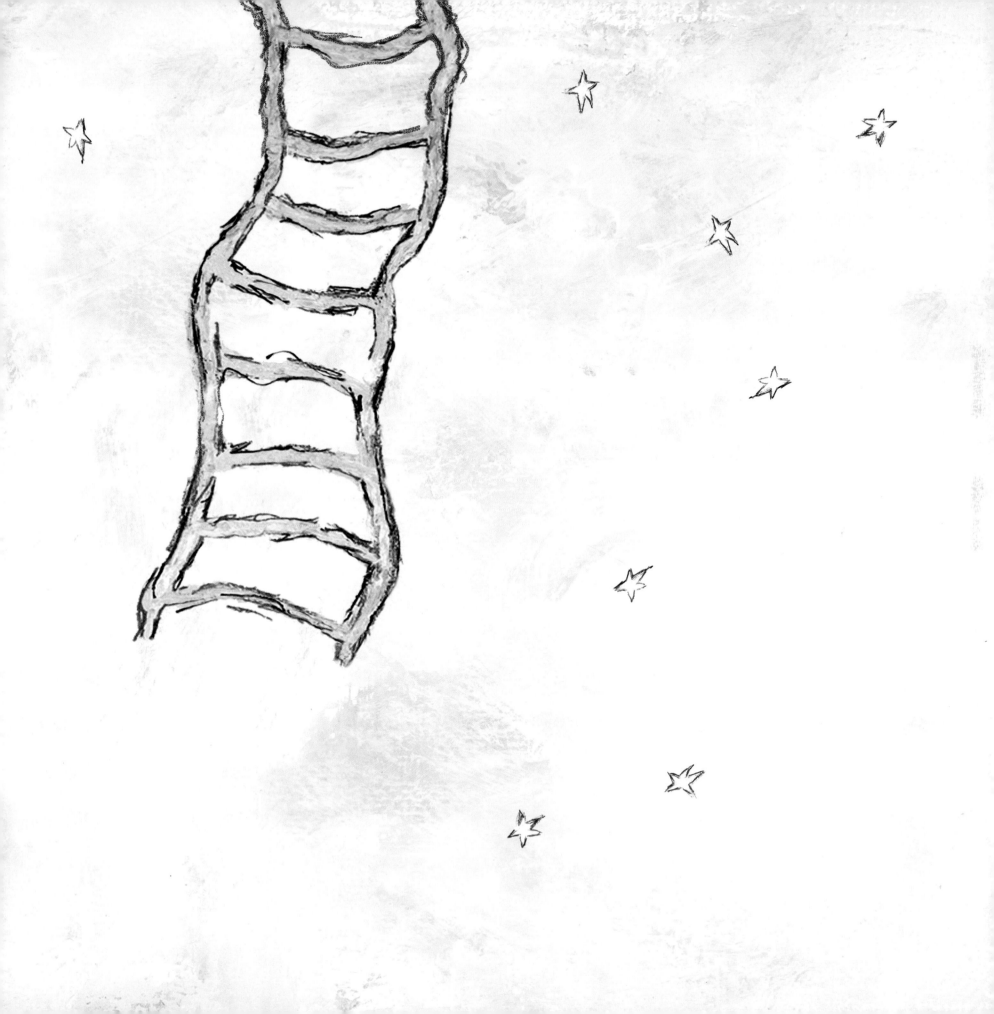

*T*HEY CELEBRATE THE TRUE ESSENCE OF WHO WE ARE

AND HAVE FAITH IN ALL THAT WE MAY BECOME.

The finer gifts

of our spirit

emerge in the

presence of their

believing hearts,

AND ALL OF OUR

HOPES AND VISIONS

ARE BORN ANEW.

OME PEOPLE AWAKEN US

TO NEW AND DEEPER REALIZATIONS,

FOR WE GAIN INSIGHT FROM

THE PASSING WHISPER OF THEIR WISDOM.

THROUGHOUT OUR LIVES

WE ARE SENT PRECIOUS SOULS

MEANT TO SHARE OUR JOURNEY.

HOWEVER BRIEF OR LASTING THEIR STAY,

THEY REMIND US WHY WE ARE HERE . . .

TO LEARN, TO TEACH, TO NURTURE . . .

TO WALK OUR PATH WITH GENTLE FOOTSTEPS,

WITH KINDNESS AND WITH LISTENING HEARTS . .

TO GIVE ALL THAT WE CAN GIVE,

TO TAKE THE LEAP OF FAITH,

AND TO RECEIVE LOVE'S BOUNTY . . .

TO VALUE

THE TREASURE

OF PROFOUND

KINSHIPS

AND THE

POWER

OF CARE . . .

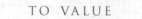

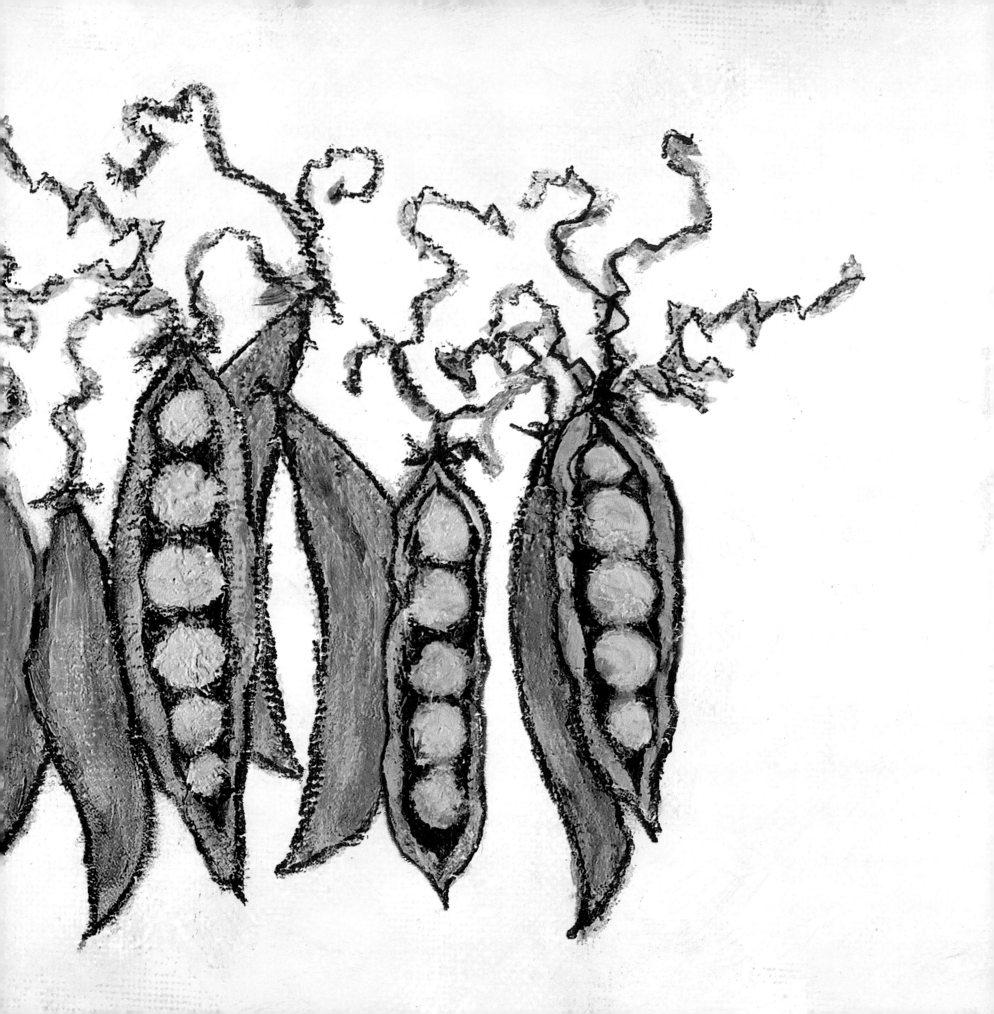

TO EMBRACE HELLOS, AND SOMETIMES GOODBYES . . .

FOR THEY ARE EACH A PART OF THE JOURNEY.

$\mathcal{S}$OME PEOPLE COME INTO OUR LIVES BY CHANCE,

OR MAYBE NOT REALLY BY CHANCE.

PERHAPS IN DESTINY'S GRAND DESIGN

THERE ARE NO RANDOM MEETINGS

AND ALL IS MEANT TO BE.

WHEN SOMEONE CARES ENOUGH

TO LOOK BENEATH OUR LAYERS,

TO LOVE US IN OUR PERFECTLY IMPERFECT FORM,

THEY GIVE US BACK THE FAITH WE WERE BORN WITH.

THEY REINTRODUCE US TO OURSELVES.

ONCE WE HAVE BEEN GRACED

BY THE RICHNESS

OF ANOTHER'S HEART,

WE COME TO LEARN

THE DIVINE CAPACITY

OF THE·HUMAN SPIRIT.

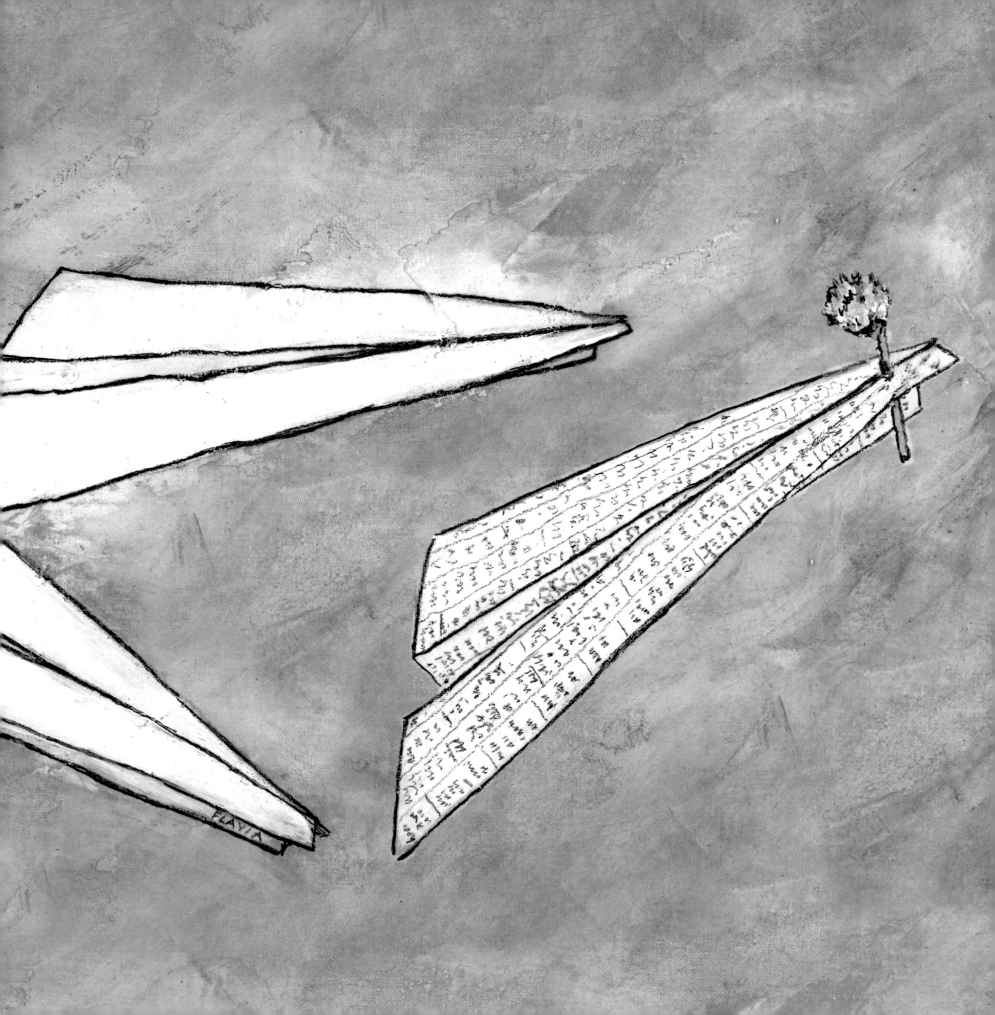

$\mathcal{W}$E DISCOVER THAT THE SHARING OF FEELINGS

CONNECTS US ALL WITHIN GOD'S MAGICAL PLAN.

IT GIVES US REASON TO BELIEVE.

$\mathcal{T}$O BELIEVE IS TO EMBRACE

THE VALUE OF A NURTURING HEART,

THE INNOCENCE OF A CHILD'S EYES,

AND THE BEAUTY OF AN AGING HAND,

FOR IT IS THROUGH THEIR TEACHINGS

THAT WE LEARN HOW TO LOVE.

To BELIEVE CAN BECOME

THE MOST PASSIONATE TREASURE WE POSSESS,

FOR IT IS TO TRUST IN THE MIRACLE OF LIVING

AND IN THE BEAUTY OF ONE ANOTHER.

To BELIEVE IS TO FIND THE STRENGTH AND COURAGE

THAT LIVES WITHIN US WHEN IT IS TIME

TO PICK UP THE PIECES AND BEGIN AGAIN . . .

IT IS TO KNOW THAT EVERY DAY IS A NEW BEGINNING,

MADE RICHER BY ALL THAT HAS COME BEFORE.

O BELIEVE IS TO HAVE FAITH,

WHICH IS TO KNOW WE ARE NEVER ALONE.

$\mathcal{W}$E ARE EACH A PART OF ALL THAT SURROUNDS US,

A PART OF ONE ANOTHER,

CONNECTED BY THE VAST MIRACLE OF LIFE ITSELF.

*S*OME PEOPLE CAPTURE OUR SOULS

IN SUCH SUBLIME AND SOOTHING WAYS,

THEY BECOME A BEACON OF HOPE.

THEY CAST A STEADY LIGHT

UPON OUR PATH AND GUIDE OUR EVERY STEP.

THEIR SHINING BELIEF IN US

HELPS US TO BELIEVE IN OURSELVES.

THIS GIFT OF LOVE WILL FOREVER BE A PART OF US . . .

AND THE CONCEPT OF FOREVER IS NOW FATHOMABLE,

FOR TIME HAS NO MEANING IN MATTERS OF THE HEART.

*W*HEN WE CARE DEEPLY ABOUT SOMEONE,

WE LEARN THE REAL GIFTS FOUND IN TIME . . .

AND THAT ITS TRUE MEASURE OF VALUE

IS DISCOVERED NOT IN ITS DURATION,

BUT IN THE SHARING OF ITS MOMENTS.

*W*E BECOME AWARE OF

HOW BRIEF AND FRAGILE LIFE CAN BE,

AND WE RECOGNIZE THERE IS NO TIME

TO LEAVE IMPORTANT WORDS UNSAID

OR DEEDS UNDONE.

*W*E UNDERSTAND THAT ALTHOUGH TIME MAY BE FLEETING,

THE WARMTH OF HUMAN EXPERIENCE ENDURES.

AITH SHOWS US THAT EACH NEW DAWN

CAN BE THE MORNING OF OUR LIVES . . .

AND A SIMPLE TURN OF THE HOURGLASS

CAN CHANGE THE COURSE OF A LIFETIME.

_W_E LEARN THAT TIME IS THE SOUL OF THE WORLD . . .

AND WHEN WE CHERISH TIME, WE CHERISH LIFE.

ᴸove helps us to discover

that it is not

the understanding of life

that is really important,

BUT THE BELIEVING

IN THE GIFTS

THAT IT BRINGS.

SOME PEOPLE MOVE OUR SOULS TO SING

AND MAKE OUR SPIRITS DANCE.

THEY HELP US TO SEE THAT EVERYTHING ON EARTH

IS PART OF THE INCREDIBILITY OF LIFE AND THAT

IT IS ALWAYS THERE FOR US TO TAKE OF ITS JOY.

*L*OVE IS ALL AROUND US.

IT IS IN THE HORIZON,

IN THE MEMORIES WE CHERISH

AND ON OUR FRONT PORCH . . .

JUST WAITING FOR OUR EMBRACE.

*L*OVE EXISTS IN MANY FORMS

AND WEAVES ITS GOLDEN THREAD

INTO THE FABRIC OF OUR BEING.

*L*ove is found in enduring friendship,

when common understanding

ignites the flickering candle of our faith.

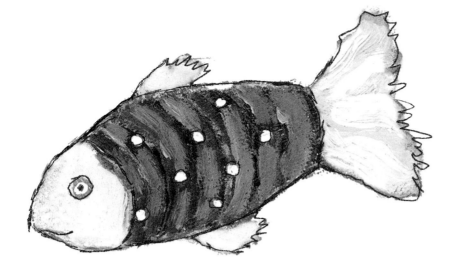

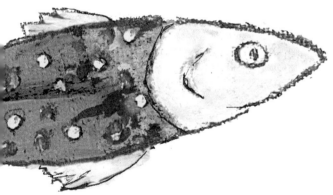
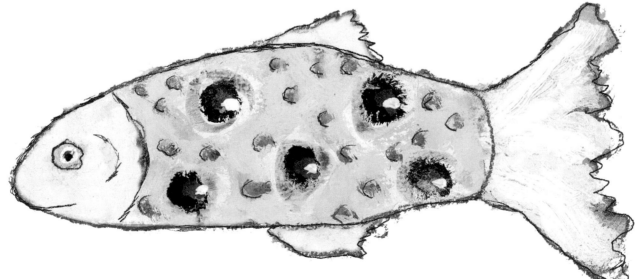

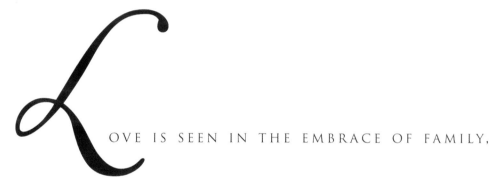

Love is seen in the embrace of family,

for in the presence of those

who share our story, we are free

to be our authentic and finest selves.

LOVE CAN BE BORN IN AN INSTANT,

WHEN AN UNEXPECTED GLANCE

FROM ACROSS A CROWDED ROOM

CAUSES OUR VERY SOUL

TO TREMBLE WITH RECOGNITION.

$\mathcal{L}$OVE CAN LIE STILL AND SILENT FOR YEARS,

THEN ONE DAY BLOSSOM

INTO PRISMS OF COLOR.

$\mathcal{L}$OVE EXISTS WITHIN OURSELVES,

AS WE REACH OUT TO OTHERS

AND FEEL THE BLISS OF GIVING . . .

FOR LOVE IS FAR RICHER IN ACTION

THAN IT EVER IS IN WORDS.

OME PEOPLE GIVE OF THEMSELVES

AND NEVER KNOW

THE DEPTH OR BREADTH

OF WHAT THEY HAVE GIVEN.

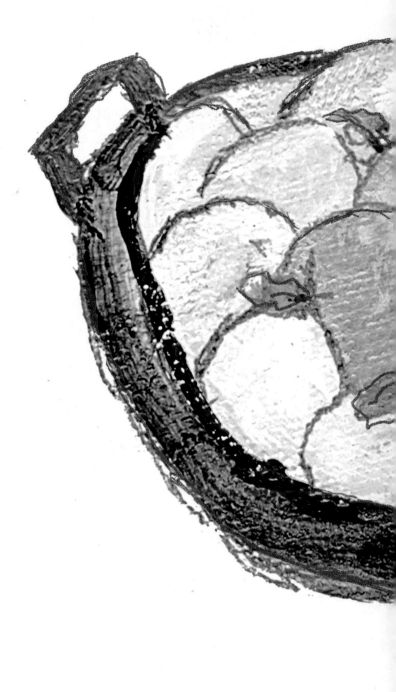

PERHAPS THIS IS

THE POWER OF LOVE

IN ITS PUREST FORM.

Because they have touched the core of our being,

we have changed and become more.

And now, all that we see and feel is measured

with a sacred reverence in honor of that love.

*T*HEIR EXISTENCE IN OUR LIVES ALLOWS US TO HOLD CLOSE

THE EVER-PRESENT BLESSING OF THIS JOURNEY WE ALL SHARE.

*S*OME PEOPLE STAY IN OUR HEARTS FOREVER.

THEY BRING TO US THE KNOWLEDGE THAT LIFE

IS A PRECIOUS OFFERING AND LOVE IS A MIRACLE

THAT BELIES THE PASSAGE OF TIME.

*W*E COME TO KNOW THAT ALL WE FEEL IN LIFE IS BORN OF LOVE . . .

EVERY HOPE,

EVERY JOY

AND SADNESS,

EVERY RAY

OF TRUTH

AND LIGHT.

*W*E ARE GIVEN A DEEPER UNDERSTANDING OF

WHAT MATTERS MOST IN THIS LIFETIME.

OME PEOPLE COME INTO OUR LIVES,

LEAVE FOOTPRINTS ON OUR HEARTS,

AND WE ARE NEVER, EVER THE SAME.

ISBN 0-7683-2093-3

Written by Flavia and Lisa Weedn
Illustrated by Flavia Weedn
© Weedn Family Trust
www.flavia.com
All rights reserved

Published in 1999 by Cedco Publishing Company
100 Pelican Way, San Rafael, California 94901
For a free catalog of other Cedco® products, please write
to the address above, or visit our website: www.cedco.com

Library of Congress Cataloging-in-Publication Data

Weedn. Flavia.
    Forever / written by Flavia & Lisa Weedn ; illustrated by Flavia Weedn.
        p. cm.
    ISBN 0-7683-2093-3
    1. Friendship   I. Weedn, Lisa, 1959-   . II. Title.
BJ1533.F8W54   1999
177' .62--DC21   99-12128
                                                                       CIP

Printed in Hong Kong

3 5 7 9 10 8 6 4

The artwork for each picture is digitally mastered using acrylic on canvas.

With love and gratitude to those talented souls who made this book a reality—
Rick Weedn, Lisa Mansfield, Diana Musacchio, Jane Durand, Tyler Tomblin,
Heather Day, Solveig Chandler, Hui-Ying Ting-Bornfreund and Annette Berlin